How to Setup a Managed Services Business in 2009

GW00394115

A soup-to-nuts guide for aspiring MSPs.

Dev Anand

AdventNet, Inc

2009 will be the best year to start a managed services business as lot of SMEs get ready to let go their one man IT shops and look for inexpensive IT providers. If you are a VAR or a system integrator thinking of starting your own managed services business, this book is for you.

Get the complete picture of how to register your business & manage federal procedures, raise working capital, cut costs on operations, win customers, and run a successful MSP business. Understand what works and what doesn't from the case studies and best practices compiled from hundreds of successful managed service providers.

Dev Anand
AdventNet, Inc

From the author

The signs are clear and visible. 2009 is going to be a year of serious recession resulting in cost cutting and downsizing across millions of companies. As companies try to squeeze every penny spent, IT budgets will vanish forcing small businesses to close down their one man IT shops and start looking out for inexpensive alternatives. This calls for a new breed of managed service providers who could offer vital IT services at a fixed and inexpensive price point. This is a great opportunity for existing VARs, System Integrators, and IT Consultants to start a managed services business.

In an effort to make this transformation smooth we present you this book - soups to nuts guide to starting an MSP business. It will give you the current trend in managed services, the sweet spot for startups, steps to register your business, plan your finances, and run an effective MSP business. We have interviewed lot of our existing customers and have compiled the best practices such as how to win new customers, why you should sell virtualization and power management, taking note of newer technologies such as Amazon Web Services and Saas based office tools etc.

We sincerely thank our customers and partners who helped us in making this guide a more effective one by sharing their views and data. We would love to know your views, send them to **devanand@adventnet.com** or **bharanikumar@adventnet.com**.

Table of Contents

CHAPTER 1

Overview

What is Managed Services?

According to Wikipedia, "Managed Services is the practice of transferring day-to-day related management responsibility as a strategic method for improved effective and efficient operations. The person or organization that owns or has direct oversight of the organization or system being managed is referred to as the client or customer. The person or organization that accepts and provides the managed service is regarded as the Managed Service Provider."

Current trend in Managed Services

Today, managed services are offered to everyone right from common man to large enterprises. If you buy a Dell Inspiron laptop or a Dell Vostro desktop you get 1 year of online backup for free. Also Dell offers remote troubleshooting as a service for a fixed price.

Lenovo too provides online backup for thinkpad series laptops in collaboration with HP. On the large scale, business giants such as IBM have already jumped into the managed services market. America's reselling giant Ingram Micro now offers managed services. But the most happening segment in managed services is the SME and it keeps growing day by day.

Who should become an MSP?

VARs (Value Added Resellers), System Integrators, IT Consultants, and sometimes traditional application service providers are the best candidates for turning into an MSP. They have the essential knowledge, skill and experience in handling IT services and solutions. If you are a VAR, then wake up. Of the lot, reports suggest that VARs have a very good potential and market to run managed services business. SMBs and Large enterprises consider them as their trusted partners as with whom they have been interacting for their IT needs.

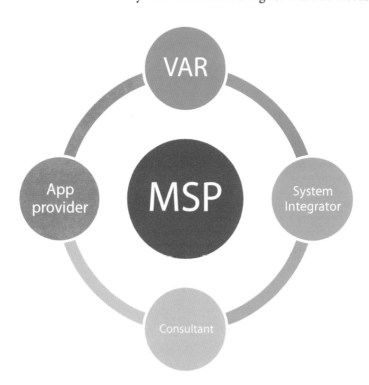

Why do MSPs have a better chance of success?

It's quite natural for one to ask this question - when every industry stalls, how could an MSP business alone be recession proof and successful? The answer lies in the unique operations model of an MSP. By having a pool of engineers who are not dedicated to any organization but work on specialized vertical functions such as networking, servers, desktops, helpdesk, and operations support an MSP could manage 10–20 companies with say 5 employees.

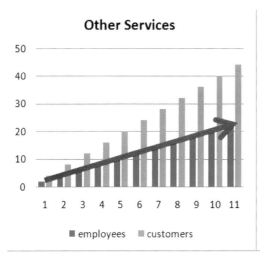

Also by centralizing the operations MSP actually shares the cost of the software/tools across a number of customers and manages a very low cost-per-device compared to an individual business owner who has to do all by him. So in short when a business owner finds it difficult to manage IT at $400–$500 per device per month, a smart and efficient MSP could do it for $100–$150 per month making it a win-win situation.

SME Managed services to boom in next five years

Industrial reports suggest that SMB managed services market is very wide open now when compared to that large enterprises. Ranging from all leading MSPs to VARs, all are eying SMB managed services market as their next big growth opportunity. SMBs, industries of 20 to 99 employees, managed services market have the potential to reach $1.6 billion by 2013. The US SMB IT managed services market alone grows to $4.3 billion by 2013. It's really a huge market to chase.

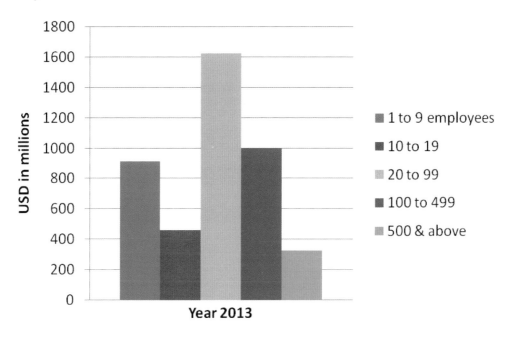

Small industries and large enterprises are not so great for offering managed services because they either lack budget or have resources to do it in-house. The best bet to pitch managed services is to businesses with 20–99 employees because they form the largest population of businesses who are tight in budget as well as dependent on IT.

Employment size of enterprise	Firms
All firms	**25,409,525**
Nonemployer firms	19,523,741
Employer firms	**5,885,784**
Firms with no employees as of March 12, but with payroll at some time during the year	802,034
Firms with 1 to 4 employees	2,777,680
Firms with 5 to 9 employees	1,043,448
Firms with 10 to 19 employees	632,682
Firms with 20 to 99 employees	526,355
Firms with 100 to 499 employees	86,538
Firms with 500 employees or more	17,047
Firms with 500 to 749 employees	5,695
Firms with 750 to 999 employees	2,709
Firms with 1,000 to 1,499 employees	2,828
Firms with 1,500 to 2,499 employees	2,281
Firms with 2,500 employees or more	3,534
Firms with 2,500 to 4,999 employees	1,739
Firms with 5,000 to 9,999 employees	905
Firms with 10,000 employees or more	890

Market Survey: Managed services market to grow big in 2009

MSPs celebrate 2009, while others mourn.

A recent market survey conducted on the MSPs revealed that the managed services market shows good potential to grow in 2009 and expects a tough competition. Majority of the MSPs who participated in the survey, believed that in 2009 their revenues will increase by 25% on an average. This is on the average 28% operating profit margins the MSPs anticipated in 2008. The projected growth rate of managed services business is 78%, according to the survey. Also majority of the MSPs said that they have made their revenues by focusing on a single industry.

The most popular industry for MSPs was Financial services (37%) followed by health care (36%), professional services (30%) etc in 2008. For 2009, among the popular industries Manufacturing (78%) ranks first and is followed by government/educational/non-profit (52%), health care (42%) etc.

(Continue)

Popular Industry types for MSPs

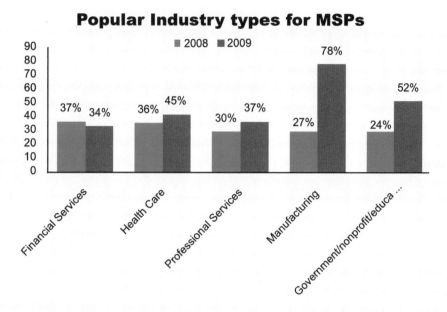

According to the survey, pricing techniques, services offered, understanding customer needs etc. (discussed at later part of the guide) are the key factors that are responsible for their success. The survey also suggests that

What are the chances of small MSPs surviving competition?

Managed services business is still very much a regional game. If you offer enough value to your customers it is unlikely that a national player would eat into your business simply because a local player can be quick as well as cost-effective. It's no different than the situation below. Guess who would you call? Obviously Joe, right? You might buy a car that is made in any part of the globe but when it comes to service, and especially break-fix, proximity plays a big role.

CHAPTER 2

Before you get started – Identify your target market first

Start small. Think local.

Today some businesses have a global foot print. But none of them were started that way. Invariably everyone started as a small local business with a very small footprint. That's exactly how you should be starting your MSP journey too. So, first define your **geographic coverage** of your business. Are you going to be the new MSP of Orlando or New York?

It's important to start local because it's easy to serve 10 customers in one city than half of them in multi-cities. Costs incurred in meeting them for winning a new business and onsite visits would work out cheaper with local customers in the long run. Moreover at the initial stages of starting a business you should spend a lot of time on meeting customers than travelling.

Start small. Think local

Double check your choice

Get the list ready

Generate leads online

Double check your choice

Don't just start a business in a city X just because you live there. Double check if the city/ state has enough number of small and medium businesses matching your target customer profile. The best way to go about doing this is get the published data on government websites/ journals. The bar graph below shows the number of businesses in each US state.

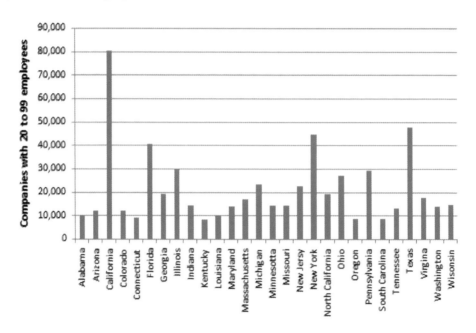

Get the list ready

Once you have defined your desired footprint start building the list of such potential businesses. There are many ways to get this done.

1. Go to the local chamber of commerce in your region and get the list of registered businesses

2. Gather public information through Google local

3. Explore associations for verticals such as finance, auto, healthcare in your region and pick up businesses

4. Rent lists from direct marketing organizations

5. Participate in industry specific trade shows and meet people

6. Mine data from your old businesses to see if any potential businesses

7. Get the sales leads from online Business Sales Leads providers.

The list you collect will serve as a master database of people you need to contact in this new business. You can maintain this list in a sophisticated CRM or a contact management tool which you would further use for campaigns or you can simply have them in an excel sheet for reference.

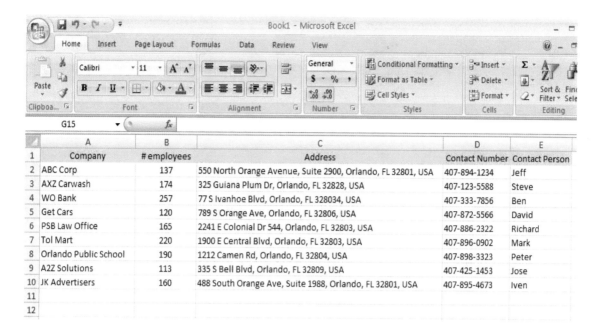

Generate leads online

A simple and quick way to generate leads is through online leads vendors (see list below). Just open an account with any of these vendors and start marketing your services. You can get the leads list sliced-and-diced matching your target customer profile. For example you can get the list of leads in California, within SFO, with employees ranging from 100–200 and specific to an industry with a certain revenue range.

Online leads vendors	Price
Lead 411 www.lead411.com	Starts from $29.95/month
GoLeads www.goleads.com	Starts from $9.95/month
InfoUSA www.infousa.com	Contact the vendor
Zapdata www1.zapdata.com	Contact the vendor
Eastcoe Databases www.eastcoedatabases.com	Starts from $99.95/month
The Top Lead Shop www.thetopleadshop.com	Starts from $17/month

Some of these tools provide an inbuilt CRM so that you can send emails to the target customers right from the website without having to install your own contact management or customer relationship software such as ACT. Companies such as Goleads.com offer a free search which gives you the count of the search you do (not the lead list but the total count of leads matching your search criteria) which could be good trial before you pay for any of these tools.

CHAPTER 3

Identify what they need (what services can you offer them?)

Know what (services) your customers need

Businesses require different kinds of services depending on their IT infrastructure. For example a design house with 50 employees would require basic desktop management whereas a bank with 100 employees would require special security services, server management, and application management. The diagram below depicts the services required against some of the critical IT components.

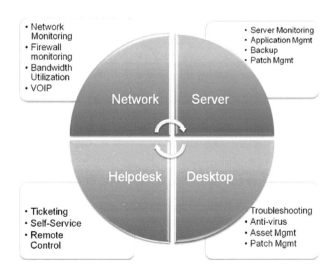

- Network Monitoring
- Firewall monitoring
- Bandwidth Utilization
- VOIP

- Server Monitoring
- Application Mgmt
- Backup
- Patch Mgmt

Network   Server

Helpdesk   Desktop

- Ticketing
- Self-Service
- Remote Control

- Troubleshooting
- Anti-virus
- Asset Mgmt
- Patch Mgmt

It's quite natural that each customer has different requirements. First understand the IT requirements of a customer like what services he/she requires whether server monitoring, security management, asset management and what type of monitoring required whether 24/7, 24/5 or 12/5 etc., Also understand if he wants to have SLAs and if so what type of SLA whether availability SLA (uptime), performance SLA (packet loss & latency) or helpdesk SLA (response time in replying to the tickets). After understanding these requirements provide your customers the optimum services.

By providing the services that do not meet the demands of a customer drags you from identifying the fault in his/her IT and in such cases chances are more for the customer to quit your service. For instance, if ABC Corp wants to manage their IT, first take a blue print of their IT and identify how many servers, desktops, routers etc., are available. Then decide on what services to offer and what type of monitoring is required.

Sample

For example let's assume that ABC Corporation operates in your region with 132 employees. The services that they require are shown below.

	Company	IT Infrastructure	IT needs	Monitoring Required	SLA
1					
2	ABC Corp	25 servers	Server monitoring Response time, Memory utilized, Patch scan etc.	24*7	99.6% uptime
3		100 desktops	Desktop management Desktop monitoring, security management, patch scan, asset management etc.	8*5	-
4		2 routers	router monitoring ping, packet loss, traffic monitoring etc.	24*7	-
5		10 printers	printer monitoring Response time, traffic monitoring etc.	8*5	99.6% uptime

Case study   AaSys Group. Managing 75 Banks with MSP Center Plus

AaSys Group is a leading managed service provider in Florida. They have been using MSP Center Plus to manage more than 75 banks in and around Florida region.

AaSys' services include everything from consulting, networking, to maintenance for banking organizations. As part of their network services, AaSys manages the server infrastructure across these banks that run to thousands of servers and infrastructure devices.

Miguel Hablutzel
AaSys Group, Inc
www.aasysgroup.com

CHAPTER 4

Get Started. Register your business first.

If you already have registered your company you may skip this section...

Checklist for registering a business

- Selecting an appropriate business structure
- Registering your business
- Getting your EIN
- Choosing a tax year
- Choosing your accounting method
- Submitting the form I-9 and W-4 filled out by your employees

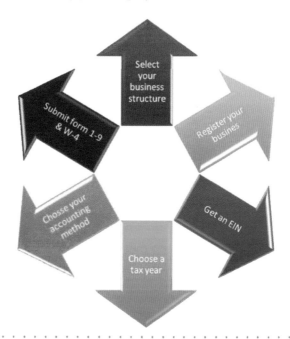

Start small. Think local

Double check your choice

Get the list ready

Generate leads online

Step 1: Selecting an appropriate business structure

When beginning a managed services business, you must decide what form of business entity to establish. Your form of business determines which income tax return form you have to file. The most common forms of business are the sole proprietorship, partnership, corporation, S corporation and Limited Liability Company (LLC). Legal and tax considerations enter into selecting a business structure.

Step 2: Registering your business

Registration is mandatory for running your business, filing income tax returns, getting copy rights etc., To register your business you must file articles of incorporation, designate a registered agent, other required documents and send the appropriate filing fee to the Division of Corporation of the State.

For instance, if you are registering a business in Florida you may require an entity to register not only at the State level but also with the local county government. Corporate entities are usually required to register with the Division of Corporations, while many professions are required to register with the Department of Business and Professional Regulation. County occupational licenses are usually obtained from the local county government.

To form a Florida corporation (profit) you must file articles of incorporation, designate a registered agent and send the appropriate filing fee to the Division of Corporations. The forms are available at http://form.sunbiz.org/cor_form.html. Download the forms (Profit corporations) and submit to the Division of Corporations in Florida.

On line registration

Another easy way of registering your business is through online incorporation service providers. You can directly log in to their website and fill your details and get your business registered.

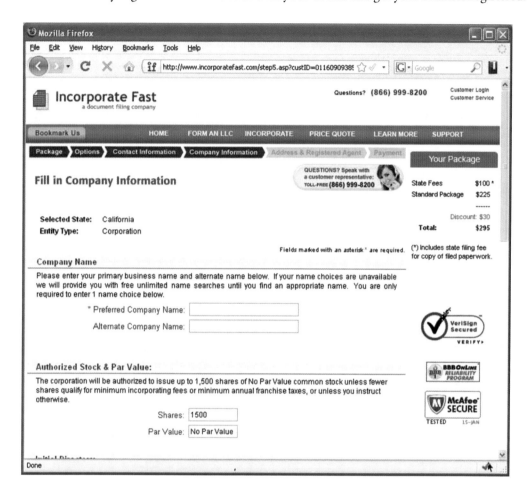

Some of the available online incorporation service provides and their charges are given in the following table.

Online Incorporation Service Provider	Charges
Incorporate Fast www.incorporatefast.com	Registration price varies according to the state. $165 for processing and registration in Florida.
Florida Incorporation Service www.floridaincorporationservice.com	$72.5 for registration (only in Florida).
My New Venture www.mynewventure.com	$159 for processing + state filing fee. (For filing in Florida $159+$80).
Incorporate Time www.incorporatetime.com	Registration price varies according to the state. $160 for processing and registration in Florida.

Step 3: Obtaining Employer Identification Number (EIN)

After registering your business obtain an Employer Identification Number (EIN). An EIN is a unique nine digit number issued by Internal Revenue System (IRS) to the business corporations for tax purposes. EIN is also known as the Tax Identification Number (TIN), Federal Employer Identification Number (FEIN) or Federal Tax Identification Number (FTIN). When the nine digit number is used for identification rather than employment tax reporting, it is usually referred to as a TIN, and when used for the purposes of reporting employment taxes, it is usually referred to as an EIN.

To obtain an EIN go to the following link https://sa.www4.irs.gov/modiein/individual/index.jsp and fill the application. After all validations are done you will get your EIN immediately upon completion. This application will be available during the following hours:

Monday - Friday: 6:00 a.m. to 12:30 a.m. Eastern time
Saturday: 6:00 a.m. to 9:00 p.m. Eastern time
Sunday: 7:00 p.m. to 12:00 a.m. Eastern time

Step 4: Choosing your tax year

You must figure your taxable income on the basis of a tax year and file an income tax return. A "tax year" is an annual accounting period for keeping records and reporting income and expenses. An annual accounting period does not include a short tax year. The tax years you can use are:

- **Calendar year** - A calendar tax year is 12 consecutive months beginning January 1 and ending December 31.
- **Fiscal year** - A fiscal tax year is 12 consecutive months ending on the last day of any month except December. A 52–53-week tax year is a fiscal tax year that varies from 52 to 53 weeks but does not have to end on the last day of a month.

Unless you have a required tax year, you adopt a tax year by filing your first income tax return using that tax year. A required tax year is a tax year required under the Internal Revenue Code and the Income Tax Regulations. You have not adopted a tax year if you merely did any of the following.

- Filed an application for an extension of time to file an income tax return.
- Filed an application for an employer identification number.
- Paid estimated taxes for that tax year.

If you file your first tax return using the calendar tax year and you later begin business as a sole proprietor, become a partner in a partnership, or become a shareholder in an S corporation, you must continue to use the calendar year unless you get IRS approval to change it or are otherwise allowed to change it without IRS approval.

Generally, anyone can adopt the calendar year. However, if any of the following apply, you must adopt the calendar year.

- You keep no books or records;
- You have no annual accounting period;
- Your present tax year does not qualify as a fiscal year; or
- You are required to use a calendar year by a provision of the Internal Revenue Code or the Income Tax Regulations.

Short Tax Year

A short tax year is a tax year of less than 12 months. A short period tax return may be required when you (as a taxable entity):

- Are not in existence for an entire tax year, or
- Change your accounting period.

Tax on a short period tax return is figured differently for each situation.

Not in Existence Entire Year

Even if you (a taxable entity) were not in existence for the entire year, a tax return is required for the time you were in existence. Requirements for filing the return and figuring the tax are generally the same as the requirements for a return for a full tax year (12 months) ending on the last day of the short tax year.

Step 5: Choosing your accounting method

Each taxpayer (business or individual) must figure taxable income on an annual accounting period called a tax year. The calendar year is the most common tax year. Other tax years are a fiscal year and a short tax year.

Each taxpayer must also use a consistent accounting method, which is a set of rules for determining when to report income and expenses. The most commonly used accounting methods are the cash method and an accrual method. Under the cash method, you generally report income in the tax year you receive it and deduct expenses in the tax year you pay them. Under an accrual method, you generally report income in the tax year you earn it, regardless of when payment is received, and deduct expenses in the tax year you incur them, regardless of when payment is made

Step 6: Submitting forms I-9 and W-4 filled by your employees

The Employment Eligibility Verification Form I-9 is a U.S. Citizenship and Immigration Services form. It is used by an employer to verify an employee's identity and to establish that the worker is eligible to accept employment in the United States. The United States government requires that all employees and employers attest to employee eligibility to work by filling out and maintaining a Form I-9 for each employee. To download the form, visit the following URL http://www.uscis.gov/files/form/I-9.pdf.

Form W-4 is a federal tax form is required by IRS and must be filled out by new employees before they receive their first paycheck. Filers must indicate the number of personal allowances they are taking, including dependents, to determine how much money will be withheld for payroll taxes. To download the form, visit the following URL http://www.irs.gov/pub/irs-pdf/fw4.pdf.

Form W-4 (2008)

Purpose. Complete Form W-4 so that your employer can withhold the correct federal income tax from your pay. Consider completing a new Form W-4 each year and when your personal or financial situation changes.

Exemption from withholding. If you are exempt, complete only lines 1, 2, 3, 4, and 7 and sign the form to validate it. Your exemption for 2008 expires February 16, 2009. See Pub. 505, Tax Withholding and Estimated Tax.

Note. You cannot claim exemption from withholding if (a) your income exceeds $900 and includes more than $300 of unearned income (for example, interest and dividends) and (b) another person can claim you as a dependent on their tax return.

Basic Instructions. If you are not exempt, complete the **Personal Allowances Worksheet** below. The worksheets on page 2 adjust your withholding allowances based on itemized deductions, certain credits,

adjustments to income, or two-earner/multiple job situations. Complete all worksheets that apply. However, you may claim fewer (or zero) allowances.

Head of household. Generally, you may claim head of household filing status on your tax return only if you are unmarried and pay more than 50% of the costs of keeping up a home for yourself and your dependent(s) or other qualifying individuals. See Pub. 501, Exemptions, Standard Deduction, and Filing Information, for information.

Tax credits. You can take projected tax credits into account in figuring your allowable number of withholding allowances. Credits for child or dependent care expenses and the child tax credit may be claimed using the **Personal Allowances Worksheet** below. See Pub. 919, How Do I Adjust My Tax Withholding, for information on converting your other credits into withholding allowances.

Nonwage income. If you have a large amount of nonwage income, such as interest or dividends, consider making estimated tax

payments using Form 1040-ES, Estimated Tax for Individuals. Otherwise, you may owe additional tax. If you have pension or annuity income, see Pub. 919 to find out if you should adjust your withholding on Form W-4 or W-4P.

Two earners or multiple jobs. If you have a working spouse or more than one job, figure the total number of allowances you are entitled to claim on all jobs using worksheets from only one Form W-4. Your withholding usually will be most accurate when all allowances are claimed on the Form W-4 for the highest paying job and zero allowances are claimed on the others. See Pub. 919 for details.

Nonresident alien. If you are a nonresident alien, see the Instructions for Form 8233 before completing this Form W-4.

Check your withholding. After your Form W-4 takes effect, use Pub. 919 to see how the dollar amount you are having withheld compares to your projected total tax for 2008. See Pub. 919, especially if your earnings exceed $130,000 (Single) or $180,000 (Married).

Personal Allowances Worksheet (Keep for your records.)

A	Enter "1" for **yourself** if no one else can claim you as a dependent	A ____
B	Enter "1" if: { • You are single and have only one job; or • You are married, have only one job, and your spouse does not work; or • Your wages from a second job or your spouse's wages (or the total of both) are $1,500 or less. }	B ____
C	Enter "1" for your **spouse**. But, you may choose to enter "-0-" if you are married and have either a working spouse or more than one job. (Entering "-0-" may help you avoid having too little tax withheld.)	C ____
D	Enter number of **dependents** (other than your spouse or yourself) you will claim on your tax return	D ____
E	Enter "1" if you will file as **head of household** on your tax return (see conditions under **Head of household** above) .	E ____
F	Enter "1" if you have at least $1,500 of **child or dependent care expenses** for which you plan to claim a credit . .	F ____
	(**Note.** Do **not** include child support payments. See Pub. 503, Child and Dependent Care Expenses, for details.)	
G	**Child Tax Credit** (including additional child tax credit). See Pub. 972, Child Tax Credit, for more information. • If your total income will be less than $58,000 ($86,000 if married), enter "2" for each eligible child. • If your total income will be between $58,000 and $84,000 ($86,000 and $119,000 if married), enter "1" for each eligible child plus "1" **additional** if you have 4 or more eligible children.	G ____
H	Add lines A through G and enter total here. **Note.** This may be different from the number of exemptions you claim on your tax return. ▶	H ____
	For accuracy, complete all worksheets that apply. { • If you plan to **itemize or claim adjustments to income** and want to reduce your withholding, see the **Deductions and Adjustments Worksheet** on page 2. • If you have more than one job or are married and you and your spouse both work and the combined earnings from all jobs exceed $40,000 ($25,000 if married), see the **Two-Earners/Multiple Jobs Worksheet** on page 2 to avoid having too little tax withheld. • If **neither** of the above situations applies, **stop here** and enter the number from line H on line 5 of Form W-4 below. }	

Cut here and give Form W-4 to your employer. Keep the top part for your records.

Form W-4 | **Employee's Withholding Allowance Certificate** | OMB No. 1545-0074 **2008**

Department of the Treasury / Internal Revenue Service ▶ Whether you are entitled to claim a certain number of allowances or exemption from withholding is subject to review by the IRS. Your employer may be required to send a copy of this form to the IRS.

1	Type or print your first name and middle initial.	Last name	2 Your social security number

Home address (number and street or rural route)	3 ☐ Single ☐ Married ☐ Married, but withhold at higher Single rate. **Note.** If married, but legally separated, or spouse is a nonresident alien, check the "Single" box.	
City or town, state, and ZIP code	4 If your last name differs from that shown on your social security card, check here. You must call 1-800-772-1213 for a replacement card. ▶ ☐	

5	Total number of allowances you are claiming (from line H above or from the applicable worksheet on page 2)	5 ____
6	Additional amount, if any, you want withheld from each paycheck	6 $ ____
7	I claim exemption from withholding for 2008, and I certify that I meet **both** of the following conditions for exemption. • Last year I had a right to a refund of **all** federal income tax withheld because I had **no** tax liability **and** • This year I expect a refund of **all** federal income tax withheld because I expect to have **no** tax liability. If you meet both conditions, write "Exempt" here ▶	7 ____

Under penalties of perjury, I declare that I have examined this certificate and to the best of my knowledge and belief, it is true, correct, and complete.

Employee's signature (Form is not valid unless you sign it.) ▶ _____ Date ▶ _____

8	Employer's name and address (Employer: Complete lines 8 and 10 only if sending to the IRS.)	9 Office code (optional) 10 Employer identification number (EIN)

For Privacy Act and Paperwork Reduction Act Notice, see page 2.   Cat. No. 10220Q   Form **W-4** (2008)

CHAPTER 5

Finances

Plan your finances

While running your business you would be spending majority of your money on people, facility, hardware, and software. Some of the major components that you would have to account for while planning your finances are given below.

Salary

Salaries range from $50k to $70k per year for a typical MSP technician in Florida.

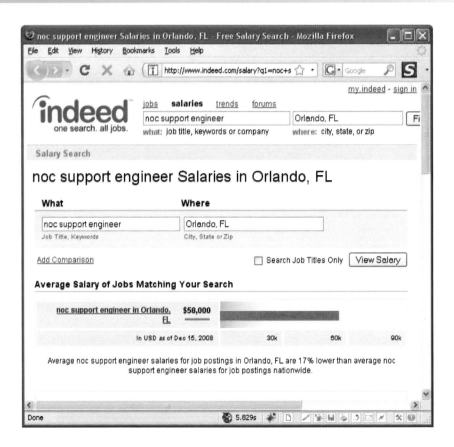

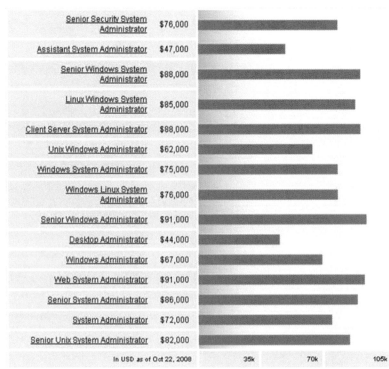

Other roles and responsibilities in a typical MSP Organization

Role	Activities
Sales & Marketing team	Makes cold calls Generates leads Closes sales
Account Manager	Single point of contact with the customer Comprehensive knowledge on all the services that you offer Prices of the services offered Ensures all the necessary contract, SLA documents are received from the customers Ensures whether the bills are sent properly and the customer pays them in time Conducting meetings to discuss and solve customer issues on contract, SLAs etc.
Engineers	Perform Root Cause Analysis (RCA) on the customer issues Changing Network configurations according to client issues Perform Core hardware and software upgrades Upgrading Switches, Routers OS Deploying critical patches Taking Periodical backups
Client Services	Provide support to clients on all aspects of account administration and client support Preparing all the necessary documents for the customer's account establishment and maintenance Ensure whether right services are provided
Helpdesk	Attends the customer requests, via voice or mail Provides solutions to the customers Assigns tickets to Operations support for analysis
Operations support	Works on the tickets raised Analyses the customer's devices remotely Fixes the issues Raises Service Request, for onsite visits
Technicians	Attends the service requests Goes onsite for replacing hardware, changing network connections etc. Raises Timesheets for onsite claims

Non-salary components

Typically the non-salary components such as insurance, 401k etc account to $10,000 per employee per year.

Lease

Lease rates vary from state to state. The average lease rate is around $5–$10 per square feet per month.

Operations

Operations include telephones, internet, power, housekeeping, stationary, food etc. For a typical small business the cost of operations would be around $5000 per employee per month.

Hardware

Hardware includes the equipments required to run business such as computers, servers, networking gears, and telephones. On an average it would cost around $2000 per employee (onetime) for setting up the hardware.

Software

Go through the below table to know the various tools that are available in the market, what solution they provide and how much do they cost.

Software	Solution offered	Price
MSP Center Plus www.mspcenterplus.com	Integrated MSP Platform.	$25 device/year
OpManager OnDemand www.ondemand.opmanager.com	Hosted monitoring tool	Contact the vendor.
Kaseya www.kaseya.com	Desktop/Server management	$120 device
Microsoft system center www.microsoft.com/systemcenter/	Desktop management	Contact the vendor.
ConnectWise www.connectwise.com	Professional Service Automation (PSA)	Contact the vendor.
N-able www.n-able.com	Network monitoring	$99 user/month
Zenith www.zenithinfotech.com	Desktop management	Contact the vendor.
Solarwinds www.solarwinds.com	Network monitoring	$2475 - 100 devices/year
Whatsup Gold www.whatsupgold.com	Server and application monitoring	$65 device/year
Autotask www.autotask.com	Professional Service Automation (PSA)	$275 - 5users/month $ 55 additional user/month

(Continue)

(Continued)

Dell EverDream www.everdream.com	Desktop management	Contact the vendor.
LogMeIn www.logmein.com	Remote control	$69.95 device/year
ScriptLogic www.scriptlogic.com	Desktop management	$23.79 device/year
Go to my PC www.gotomypc.com	Remote control	$14.95 device/month
VNC www.realvnc.com	Remote control	$50 per host
Level Platforms www.levelplatforms.com	Network monitoring	Contact the vendor.

Marketing

Marketing and business development expenses vary from company to company but it is safe to assume at least a minimum of $100,000 per year to be spent on this avenue.

Cost of running a 5 member organization

Let's assume that you have 5 employees and you have a small office where you run your operations center then the cost incurred per year would be as shown below.

Item	Description	Cost (annual)
Salary	System Administrators – 3 Backend operations support Sales and marketing – 1– 1	$380,000 [3*$80k, 1*$50k, 1*$90k]
Non-salary components such as insurance etc	On an average around $20k per employee is spent on these non-salary components.	$100,000
Facility lease/rental	Minimum 100 square feet is required per employee. At an average rate of $1.5 per sqft per month for lease you will be shelling our $750 per month on lease.	$9,000
Operations	Other facilities include telephones, air conditioning, internet, housekeeping, power etc.	$60,000

(Continue)

Item	Description	Cost (annual)
Hardware	Computers for 4 operations (System admin-3 & backend operations-1) team. Laptop for sales. Servers for hosting product. Networking gear.	$13,500 [4*2000, 1*$1000, $2500, $2000]
Software	Includes the remote management and business software you need to run the business. (Refer the table Various tools available in the market.)	$5000
Marketing and advertising expenses	Advertisements, Website, Meeting customers, Tradeshows etc	$100,000
Total		$667,550

Go slow on hiring ...

Salary accounts to 70% of your expenses.

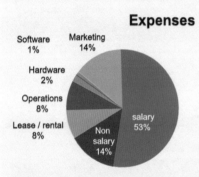

Hence it is important that you go slow on hiring and have enough customers on board before you start hiring. Till you reach that phase you should look for some frugal ways to run business. Some of our customers have handled this phase very frugally in different ways ranging from work-from-home to virtual offices.

Type	Description	Cost incurred
Working from home	If you are yet to acquire a single customer then the perfect way to get started is by working from home. Start with building a website for your business and try some free tools.	$0
Rented datacenter + work from home	If you are confident of few customers signing up with you then you might invest some money on either hosted MSP software or you run a MSP platform in a rented datacenter.	$10 per device per month Or $600 per month for hosting + cost of on-premise software
Your own bare-bones Network Operations Center operating out of a SOHO office.	If you are operating in data sensitive verticals such as banking you might have to invest more in building your own network operations center.	Approx $2500 for server hardware. Plus cost of software. Plus 100% extra for bandwidth, power, and other operations.

Raising working capital

Stop worrying about the working capital required to run your managed services business. Today various Banks are ready to offer working capital. Wells Fargo bank offers working capital loans from $5,000 to $100,000 for new business that is less than 2 years old. They require your business information such as business name, TIN, annual revenue, name and contact details of the business owner, business banking account numbers etc. They offer loan terms up to 5 years.

You can also approach for SBA loans. The SBA is a federal agency that helps established businesses grow and helps new businesses get started. SBA loans are not directly provided by the SBA, but provided by commercial lenders. SBA guarantees a portion of the amount to the lender in case the borrower fails to return.

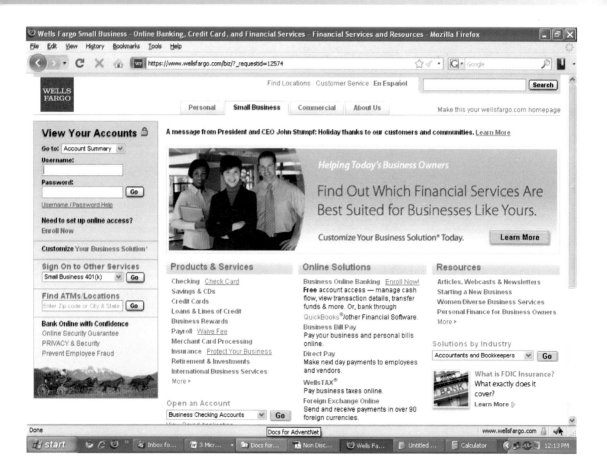

CHAPTER 6

Operations

Plan for your operations

Operations can be broadly classified into two types–internal facing and external facing. Internal facing teams work on a day-to-day basis to offer a smooth working environment for the external facing teams. The two large external facing teams are the customer service and sales. Though there are many roles described here many of them would be performed by one or two in some cases.

Departments	Description
Customer Service	This is the core team of a managed services organization. Facilitates smooth management of customer IT. Encompasses engineers, support staff, helpdesk, onsite technicians etc.
Sales and marketing	Teams that work on bringing customers to the table. Often involved in account management, marketing campaigns, advertisements etc.
Purchase	Facilitates purchasing of hardware, software, office equipments, and everything that is bought from outside.
Sysadmin	Handles day-to-day troubleshooting as well as strategic IT enhancements such as security, backup, bandwidth planning etc.
Payroll and employee benefits	Handles monthly salary processing, employee tax planning, and other activities related to employee benefits.
Housekeeping	Ensures a clean and hygienic office atmosphere taking care of every aspect of cleaning and replenishments.
Human Resources	Handles employee attendance, leaves, salary hikes, employee satisfaction etc.
Legal	Protects the company's IP rights and other investments legally by verifying all contracts and agreements signed.

Reducing internal operations headache

To reduce your operations headache you can outsource some of the non-core activities such as payroll processing. One of the leading firms that offer HR as a service is Trinet.

Services offered by Trinet	Description
HR Services	Includes all HR activities such as payroll, human capital guidance, employee related state and federal tax filing and recordkeeping etc, employee assistance, health and benefit Programs.
Human Capital Services	Offers recruiting, measuring and rewarding performance, career transition and counseling etc.
International HR	Through global relationships offers HR services in 50 countries worldwide.
Insurance	Offers extensive range of insurance coverage such as health insurance, Workers' compensation, building and personal property insurance

Reducing external operations headache

To reduce your external operation headache and cut cost better outsource your external operations to India. With a vast pool of skilled engineers there are a number of Indian IT service provider organizations waiting to do this for you for say $10 per device per month. Most of these companies have well established processes and also boast of their employee profiles – most of them with 2–5 years experience being sysadmins and network admins, with CCNA, MSCE certifications.

Sample calculation: Cost of setting up an operations support team in US Vs outsourcing. Total number of devices to be managed is 500 and number of operations support personnel required is 5. At an average salary of $55,000 per operations guy per year, you would be shelling out $275,000 on salaries for 5 operations members. And at $10 per device per month you would be able to get almost similar job done by an Indian partner for $60,000 per year. Moreover, if you have multi-year contracts the difference becomes high when you include salary increments every year.

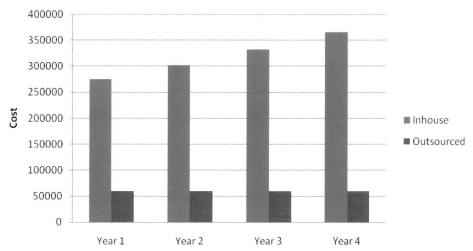

Inhouse operations vs Outsourced operations

MSP Center Plus Market Place

Many MSP Platform vendors offer operations support as part of their package itself. And few others such as MSP Center Plus brings together a market place which enables you to browse through a list of AdventNet certified IT operations provider and pick one that suits your business model.

It makes life easier for you as you don't have to go through the pains of identifying a partner and managing the relationship. In case it sucks, you will be seemlessly be handedover to a new IT operations partner through MSP Center Plus guys. Certified partnership program protects your business as it includes Non-competing and non-discloure agreements as part of the process.

Case study	Smart IMS

 Smart IMS is an innovative, rapidly growing, client-centric company that delivers high value-added IT solutions to major corporations in the U.S., Europe and Asia. Smart IMS is an AdventNet partner who is capable of offering remote monitoring, backend call support, and troubleshooting services to MSP Center customers.

Other services offered by Smart IMS include outsourcing of IT Infrastructure Support, Application Development, Packaged Application Implementation, Testing, as well as consulting.

India Office

SmartIMS (India) Ltd.
Plot No. 13,
Road No. 9, Jubilee Hills,
Hyderabad 500 035, AP, India
Tel:91-40--44335000
Email: Gayathri.Rao@SmartIMS.com

US Office

Smart IMS Inc.
103 Morgan Lane, Suite#104
Plainsboro, NJ – 08536
Tel 609-955-3030
Fax 609-936-9866
Email: Gayathri.Rao@SmartIMS.com

CHAPTER 7

Legal

Legal Documents

Legal documents define the contractual relationship between you and your customer. They provide the exact details on the rights and limitations what you and your customer have with each other. Whenever acquiring a new customer make it a process to get sign from the customer in the legal documents. In the long run only the legal documents are considered valid when any issues arise between you both.

Agreement of Services is the important legal document that you and your customers should sign whenever you acquire a new contract. The services agreement document should cover what are all the services are committed to offer, who is the liaison person, intellectual property rights, security standards, third party non disclosure agreement, validity period of this agreement and termination process of this agreement.

Agreement for Services

This **Agreement for Services** (AGREEMENT) ('the Agreement) is signed on _____, 2008, by and between:

_____

And

_____

1 Purpose and scope of this AGREEMENT:

This AGREEMENT is between _____ (hereinafter referred to as YYYYYYYY) and _____(hereinafter referred to as XXXXXXXX), wherein,   will provide monitoring services to _____ to monitor their LAN and WAN infrastructure based on the tentative proposal # _____

2 Natures of Services provided:

The services provided by _____ to _____are limited to monitoring services only. In addition _____ will provide alerting services in the form of Emails and/or SMS's only to selected staff from _____.

3 Liaisons for the _____:

_____ will nominate one or more person/s who will be the liaison person/s ("Manager/s") for specific employee provided by _____ to _____ during the term of the trial period consultant shall interact and coordinate with the Manager/s.

4 Validity period of this AGREEMENT:

This AGREEMENT is valid for a period of _____ days. The AGREEMENT can be extended with mutual agreement between _____ and _____. _____ shall provide agreed upon monitoring services to _____ for a maximum period of _____ commencing _____ weeks from the date of signature of this agreement. After the stipulated period of _____ days, monitoring services shall be automatically terminated by _____ _____ Network Management Server.

5 Commercial:

After the completion of trial period and on the basis of assessment, nature and complexity of the work _____ shall issue a comprehensive monitoring and management solution with the commercial aspects to _____.

6 Intellectual Property Rights/confidentiality agreements:

All software, systems, ideas, concept, designs, documentation or any other material produced by the _____ during the trial period to _____ will either be

Intellectual Property of _____ or that of its Customers. _____ will not have any rights to such material described as above.

7 Third Party Non-Disclosure Agreement:

_____ will keep all the data, sources and information confidential and will not disclose or release it to any other party.

_____ and their employees/sub-contractors shall not disclose any information related to _____ IT infrastructure to anybody not even to any related party unless asked by _____ to do so. The vendor/sub-contracting agencies who will be involved during the set-up for monitoring services will be held responsible for the conduct of their personnel.

_____ and their representative shall not disclose _____ or its Clients private information. This private information includes but not is limited to identified client data, employee personal data, security posture, vulnerability status, and attack status. This clause will remain valid even after the termination or expiry of this AGREEMENT.

8 Security Standards

Malicious software such as viruses can cause considerable damage to information & IT assets. _____ shall ensure that effective anti virus measures are followed across Client. _____ shall agree to enhance its guard against intrusions and failures that may affect confidentiality, availability and integrity of information and may damage information assets. _____ shall not be held responsible for any threats and damage which may emerge out of virus/malicious attack or natural or unforeseen disaster.

_____ shall meticulously try to monitor _____ infrastructure, in event of an alert not being generated by _____ Monitoring Server due to any unforeseen reason, _____ will not be responsible for any loss of data/ service that _____ accumulates.

9 Termination of this AGREEMENT:

Either party can voluntarily terminate this AGREEMENT by giving _____ days notice to the other party. If _____ terminates this AGREEMENT voluntarily, _____ shall provide all the documents and reports generated during the stipulated period of monitoring.

READ AND AGREED

On behalf of   **On behalf of**

_____   _____

Signed: _____   **Signed:**

Name: _____   **Name:**

Title: _____   **Title:**

Date: _____   **Date:**

CHAPTER 8

How to migrate from VAR to managed services?

WAR on the VARs

Gartner predicts that 40% of the VARs will go out of business if they don't switch to managed services. Shrinking margins on hardware sales, competition from direct channels, and increasing competition pushes VARs to lookout for other avenues to sustain business. Analysts and experts continue to express their opinion that the MSP model suits best for traditional VARs who sell low margin products, taking backups, replacing hardware etc. and receive unpredictable revenue from break-fix maintenance gigs.

The most compelling reason for change

Traditional VAR business often takes a cost-plus approach where the profits come from the margins on every hardware/software sale. This model is so ineffective that you always work hard for the hardware vendors and end up with stagnating/declining profits irrespective of stellar revenue growth.

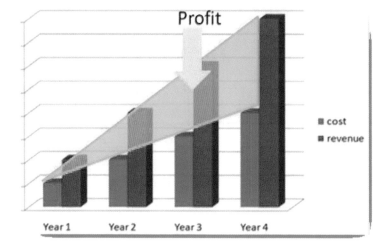

In contrast, the MSP model gives you a steady stream of recurring revenue and also enables you to increase profits over the years.

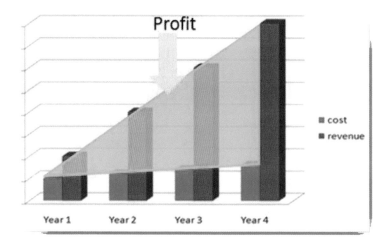

Managing change

There's no magic potion to migrate your business model from VAR to MSP. It needs a cultural change that cuts through every process and every employee in the organization. You as the president of the company need to manage this change and ensure a smooth transition from traditional business to the new managed services business.

Key doctrines that you should set for yourself for change:

Doctrine	What you need to internalize	Benefit
I am not selling products anymore.	We are no more a product–reselling company. We are a service provider by every act.	Your focus automatically shifts from vendor relations to understanding the end customers and finding ways to add value to their business with your service.
My employees won't be billed per hour.	We are no more selling human hours. We are selling a packaged service at a fixed cost per month.	Cuts your employees free to work on several customers Vs getting locked with just one customer at a time.
We will not be reactive…but proactive.	We are no more a break-fix company. We will be proactive to the maximum possible extent.	Being proactive helps you identify problems before they become business impacting downtimes.
We are selling off the trucks and buying remote tools.	No more truck rolls. Will do everything remotely and will save human capital for valuable and billable visits	Protects your investment on employees as they spend more time working than travelling.

CHAPTER 9

Winning new customers

There ain't no such thing as a FREE LUNCH

When PowerPoint presentations, lengthy discussions, and beer fail to help you win a new business, offering a FREE TRIAL does. We have seen this in most of our successful managed service provider customers where they throw-in 6 months of FREE monitoring along with a hardware installation or a server upgrade. At the end of the trial period you gain enough insight about the prospects' networks, servers, vulnerabilities, traffic patterns and potential problems that you are fully equipped to show value and win a managed services contract.

Two things they want you to talk about

Business owners are interested in just two things 1) savings you bring in to the organization and 2) hassles you take away from them. If you can strongly display these two values if am sure you can win any business deal.

#1: Show them savings

Money is the most influential influencer worldwide. So when you approach new customers, do your homework. Calculate how much the customer spends right now on managing IT and show how much he would save if it is managed by you.

There ain't no such thing as a FREE LUNCH

Two things they want you to talk about

For example, let's assume a company with 200 devices and two resources to manage it – a network administrator and a system support assistant. The bare minimum cost incurred in managing the devices in house would be around $136k per year.

Item	Details	Cost
Salary	On an average the company would be spending around $54,000 + $55,000 = $109,000 every year on salary.	$109,000
Infrastructure for managing the devices.	Other expenses spent for Network Administrator + System support assistant such as systems, amenities, blackberry etc.	$10,000
Software applications	Multiple tools for managing IT. Server monitoring tool, desktop management tool, remote management tool etc. * Assuming an average cost-per-device of 7.46 per month. 200 devices x $7.46 X 12 months	$17,904*
Total		**$136,904**

Assume that you can manage these 200 devices at $30 per device per month. That makes it $72,000 per year. At a 10% hike every year the cost of doing it in-house would touch around $635 k in four years. If the customer takes the managed services route he would save around 55%.

	In-house	Managed Services
First Year	$136,904	72,000
Second Year	$150,594	72,000
Third Year	$165,654	72,000
Fourth Year	$182,219	72,000
Total	$635,371	$288,000
Savings		$347,371
In percentage		55%

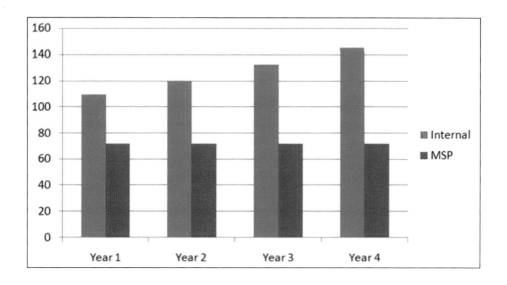

Salary.com

Salaries paid for related job responsibilities. For your reference.

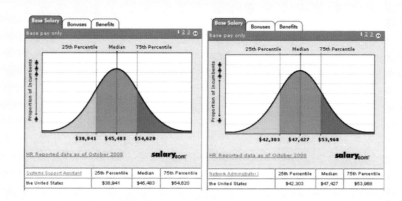

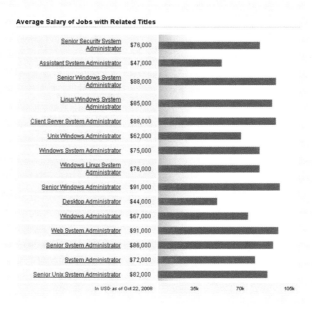

#2: Tell them they can mind their own business now

No kidding. Managing the IT (and the IT guy) for a small business owner is really a headache. It distances them from their core competency and takes away considerable amount of time.

Imagine an architectural design house with 100 employees and one IT guy. Day-to-day operations involve uploading images to the server from the user machines, backing up the images, and ensuring all machines are up and running all the time. Though it looks simple, over a period of time it brings lot of problems for the business owner.

Problems in managing the IT guy:

Problem	Description
IT guy don't get a challenging work environment in SMEs	Small organizations fail to provide IT guys with a challenging and dynamic work environment. Being geeks at heart these IT guys normally prefer to work in large enterprises where they get to be hands on with cutting edge technologies and be update.
Business owner has limited scope for increasing the salary for the IT guy	Unlike large enterprises the IT guys in SMEs have very limited chance to improve. Their work is more of a repeated kind. Business owners also have very limited scope to offer high salary as their business model varies to that of large enterprises.
Business owner needs to spend his valuable time in motivating and guiding the IT guy.	It becomes mandatory for the Business owner to motivate and guide the IT guy though he doesn't play a major role in expanding his business.

It's very clear that Business owners don't want to have an IT guy. As a MSP you could manage their IT and let him have a full focus on his core business.

Virtualization sells.
Sell Virtualization.

What is virtualization?

Computer virtualization refers to the abstraction of computer resources, such as the process of running two or more logical computer systems on one set of physical hardware. The concept originated with the IBM mainframe operating systems of the 1960s, but was commercialized for x86-compatible computers only in the 1990s. With virtualization, a system administrator could combine several physical systems into virtual machines on one single, powerful system, thereby unplugging the original hardware and reducing power and cooling consumption.

Though there are a lot of innovations happening in the desktop virtualization, we will limit the scope of this document to server virtualization. In server virtualization a single server box is partitioned into multiple virtual servers running different Operating Systems, thereby achieving higher server density. The biggest advantage of server virtualization is that with the exception of sharing the core resources, each virtual server acts as its own entity. Problems with an application on one server do not affect others, and it is possible to reboot a specific virtual server.

How virtualization helps your customers?

Virtualization is the key to increasing efficiency, ease of management, and most importantly saving costs in datacenters. Even if your customers don't ask for virtualization, explaining the advantages of it would help you persuade them towards virtualization. If you don't have virtualization in your service catalog, add it today.

Top 7 virtualization benefits that you can sell to your customers:

Benefit	Description	Value
Reduced number of physical servers	By virtualizing you can reduce the number of physical servers at your customer datacenter drastically.	Reduced maintenance costs. Reduced space.
Reduced energy consumption	Reduced number of boxes reduces the energy consumed.	Reduced energy costs.
Multiple OS on a single hardware	By virtualizing you can run multiple operating systems on a single box.	Reduced hardware costs.
Reduced downtimes	Reduced number of boxes increases effective monitoring.	Increased efficiency.
Rapid new servers deployment	Develop a standard virtualization setup and duplicate when building a new server	Reduced deployment time.
Easy disaster recovery	By virtualizing you can take periodical snapshots of servers so that in case of a sudden shutdown, you can restore the snapshot and bring up the machines.	Reduced data loss.
Improved Reliability and Availability	Application problem in one VM does not affect the other	Improved overall service availability

How much they can save?

Assume that a customer has 5 Dell Power Edge R200 servers for running Microsoft.Net, GlassFish, WebLogic, Tomcat, and Silverstream applications separately. By virtualizing you can run all the 5 applications on a single Dell Power Edge 2900 server. Go through the below given calculations to know how much your customers can by choosing virtualization.

Category	5 dedicated servers Dell Power Edge R200	1 virtualized server Dell Power Edge 2900	Savings
Hardware cost	5 * $749 = $3475	$1499	$1976. Save up to 70%
Power	5 * 345W = 1725W	930W	795W. Save up to 65%
Electricity cost 9.74 cents/kWh in Florida	1725/1000 * 8670 * 9.74/100 = $1,456	930/1000 * 8670 * 9.74/100 = $785	$761. Save up to 65%

Case study   Cornerstone IT

One of our MSP customers in New York had a customer asking them for a server upgrade. The customer was a leading law firm in New York who is also a member of MSI Global Alliance. The law firm has been employing this MSP for hardware upgrades since early days when the MSP was originally a VAR reselling hardware and software.

After a preliminary evaluation the MSP found a greater scope to Virtualize the environment which consists of 30 physical servers running in different rack holdings. When presented with the cost and space savings the customer too was impressed and gave approval for virtualization.

The final implementation was a 5 server single rack holding setup with the exact same set of services being offered. Needless to say the MSP was also offered a remote monitoring opportunity by the customer because of the faith they have in them now.

[Seen in picture: Thomas Moreo (standing) and Neil Falla of Cornerstone.IT]

Server Virtualization solutions

Some of the Server Virtualization solutions available in the market:

Vendor	Solution
Parallels	Virtuozzo Container www.parallels.com/products/virtuozzo/
VMware	VMware ESX Servers www.vmware.com/products/vi/esx/
Microsoft	Virtual Server 2005 R2 www.microsoft.com/windowsserversystem/ virtualserver/
Microsoft	Windows Server 2008 Hyper-V www.microsoft.com/windowsserver2008/en/us/ hyperv.aspx
Citrix	Xen Server Standard & Enterprise Edition www.xensource.com

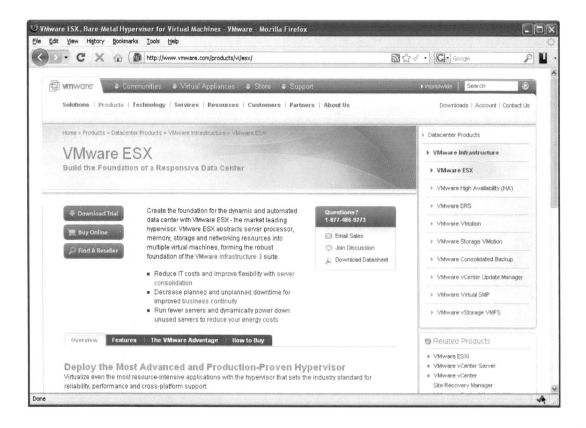

CHAPTER 11

Advocate power management – Go green

What is power management?

Automatically turning off computer components such as monitors, hard drives, CPU, and RAM after a period of inactivity is referred to as power management. All computers and laptops sold today have power management options inbuilt to switch to standby or idle mode when no operations are done. This little feature enables lot energy savings. For example, the total power consumed by a typical PC (P4, 1.75 GHz & 17" CRT monitor) is 175 watts/hour but during sleep mode it consumes only 35 watts/hr.

Why should you practice power management?

It's just unbelievable to know that CO2 emissions from just 15 computers are equivalent, in energy terms, to the gas consumption of one car. Moreover, Gartner reports that Information and communications technology (ICT) is responsible for 2% of the global CO2 emissions, an amount equivalent to aviation. Factors that contribute to the 2% are in-use phase of PCs, servers, cooling, fixed and mobile telephony, local area network (LAN), office telecommunications and printers across millions of businesses all over the world. Enabling power management on these devices will be a global imperative in the near future.

As an MSP you have the option to be a thought leader and start practicing power management and green computing in your customer environment for two reason – 1) it saves mother earth and 2) it saves huge amount of money for your customers.

How much can you save?

A company with 500 computers can save anywhere from $30,000 to $60,000 per year on energy bills. Assume you have a customer in FL who runs 500 Dell Vostro 200 Minis with Intel Pentium Dual Core E2160 processor and a 17" monitor. Given the retail price of 9.74 cents per kW hour in Florida, your customer would be burning 1226.4 kW hours per year and paying $60k on energy bills if all the computers were switched on 24*7.

- 65Watts + 75Watts X 8760 hours / 1000 = 1226.4 kW hours [Thermal Design Power of E2160 is 65Watts. For monitors its 75Watts.]
- 1226.4kW hours X 9.74 /100 X 500 = $59,725

If the company follows standard business hours of 9AM-6PM Monday to Friday, the total working hours contribute just 27% of the overall available time.

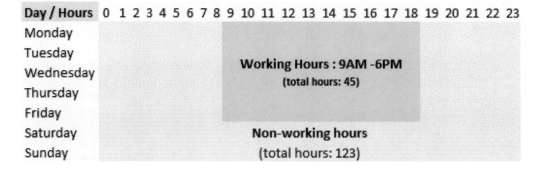

| Day / Hours | 0 | 1 | 2 | 3 | 4 | 5 | 6 | 7 | 8 | 9 | 10 | 11 | 12 | 13 | 14 | 15 | 16 | 17 | 18 | 19 | 20 | 21 | 22 | 23 |

Monday
Tuesday
Wednesday   **Working Hours : 9AM -6PM**
Thursday   (total hours: 45)
Friday
Saturday   **Non-working hours**
Sunday   (total hours: 123)

And in these 45 hours, reports indicate that, only 60% of the time the desktops are actively used. Rest goes in breaks, phone calls, meetings, and discussions. If someone enables strict power management for the above case, it will result in a savings of approximately $50k per year

- $59,725 X 0.73 = $43,599 (for non-working hours)
- $59,725 X 0.27 X 0.4 = $6,450 (for 40% idle time)
- Total: $43,599+$6,450 = $50,049

Depending on whether the computers were powered on 100% of the time or 50% of the time, the savings could vary from $50k to $29.5k per year.

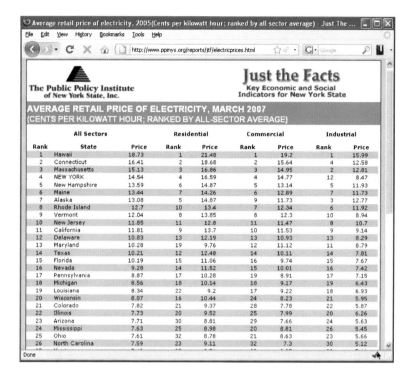

Power management in Windows

Windows offers two power management options - standby and hibernate. In standby mode the computer goes to a low power mode, with all applications and files remain open. Only the RAM part of it will be active to maintain whatever resides and consumes very minimum voltage.

In hibernate mode the computer writes off the entire contents of its real memory as one big "hiberfil.sys" and stored in the C drive. Once the writing gets completed, all power is removed from the computer, as if you have shutdown. Again when power is initiated, the computer boots and starts the applications in the startup and reads the "hiberfil.sys" file available in C drive. It proceeds to load the entire contents back.

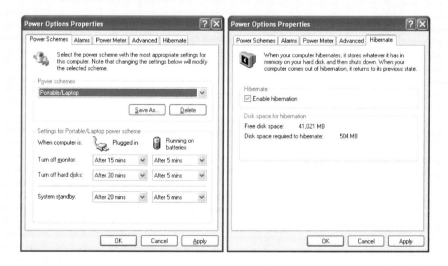

Tools that automate Windows power management

Most MSP Platforms in the market today support automating power management. This helps MSPs to go confidently to the customers and implement power management with ease. For example, MSP Center Plus enables you to configure power management options ONCE and deploy them to thousands of remote computers in just few clicks.

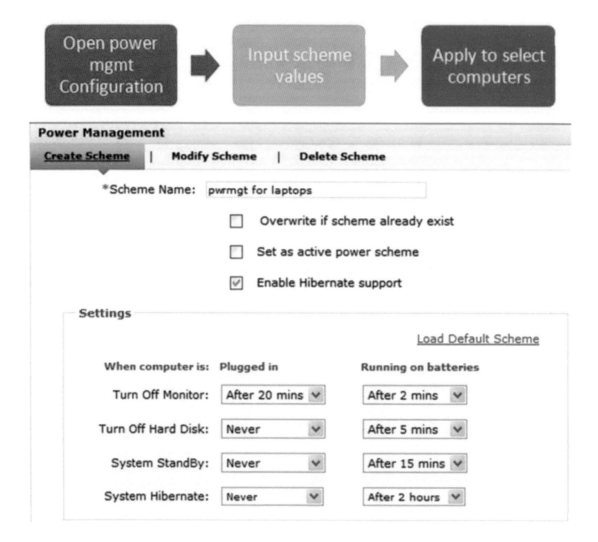

CHAPTER 12

Package your pricing

Importance of pricing

Pricing decides revenue. If you price low, you lose money, if you price high you lose customers. It's a balancing act. Managed Services is a big and everlasting opportunity and there is no need to rush up on pricing your clients. There is no need to jump on conclusions and give away discounts to your customers as it is to capture your share in the market.

Analyze your client first and look at their business, whether he is a Bank or a Healthcare firm. You should price your services based on the value you create and not entirely on cost. Converse with your customer and understand his business needs. This helps in establishing the value of your offerings to the customer. Based on this, price and sell your service.

Basic pricing models

- **Per device** – This is fairly simple and most MSPs utilize this. They develop a flat fee for each device type that is supported in the environment. E.g., $69 for Desktops, $299 per server, $29 for network printers etc. This model is easy to quote and monthly billing is simple

- **Per user** – Very similar to per device model, but the flat fee is billed per end user per month and covers for all devices used by each end user. Includes, office PC, laptops, PDAs etc.

- **All you can eat** – This is extremely flexible and includes all remote support, on-site support and provide 24/7/365 support or service. The primary goal is to provide the customer with ability to budget their IT support cost over a year's time.

Package the pricing

Provide a variety of pricing options that cover different customer's needs. Say, Silver, Gold and Platinum Packages.

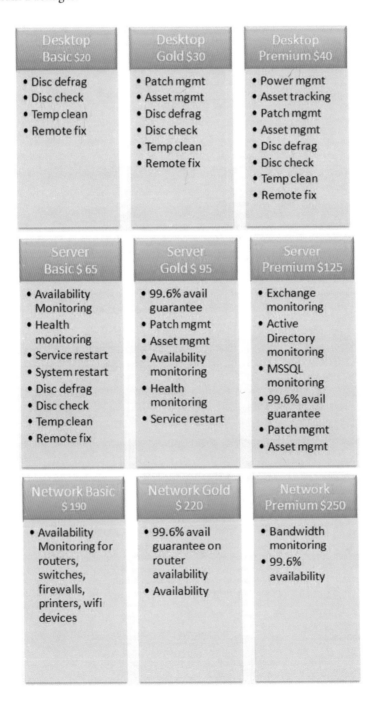

Desktop Basic $20	Desktop Gold $30	Desktop Premium $40
• Disc defrag • Disc check • Temp clean • Remote fix	• Patch mgmt • Asset mgmt • Disc defrag • Disc check • Temp clean • Remote fix	• Power mgmt • Asset tracking • Patch mgmt • Asset mgmt • Disc defrag • Disc check • Temp clean • Remote fix

Server Basic $ 65	Server Gold $ 95	Server Premium $125
• Availability Monitoring • Health monitoring • Service restart • System restart • Disc defrag • Disc check • Temp clean • Remote fix	• 99.6% avail guarantee • Patch mgmt • Asset mgmt • Availability monitoring • Health monitoring • Service restart	• Exchange monitoring • Active Directory monitoring • MSSQL monitoring • 99.6% avail guarantee • Patch mgmt • Asset mgmt

Network Basic $ 190	Network Gold $ 220	Network Premium $250
• Availability Monitoring for routers, switches, firewalls, printers, wifi devices	• 99.6% avail guarantee on router availability • Availability	• Bandwidth monitoring • 99.6% availability

CHAPTER 13

Build a service catalog, it helps

What is a service catalog?

It's a good practice to build a service catalog for your business irrespective of whether you are big or small. Service catalog is a list of services you offer to your customers. According to ITIL V3, the service catalog must be easily accessible and should be recognized as the first source of information for users seeking access to a service. It must include not only the value proposition and pricing, but also the ordering and request procedures for users, as well as standard fulfillment practices and service level agreements (SLAs) for IT service teams.

Service catalog in ITIL V3

Service catalog was introduced in ITIL v2, but it didn't offer much in depth focus. In most of the cases, the paper-based Service Catalog document went unread and unused by customers. Also IT industries which implemented SLM, had their catalog more speaking about the technical metrics associated with network and system management rather than the services offered on those performance metrics.

The new ITIL V3 Service Design book found the solution. It removes Service Catalog responsibilities from Service Level Management (SLM) process and promotes the Service Catalog from a simple listing of services into its own process the

Service Catalog Management (SCM) process. The Service Catalog is the output of the SCM process and includes all the services offered.

ITIL also suggests that users must be provided with a self-service portal in the Service Catalog, as their primary interface for requesting new IT services and obtaining status of service requests. Thereby it introduced a new process called Request Fulfillment process to standardize the handling of service requests. The Request Fulfillment process acknowledges the fact that most of the work done by IT is repetitive and inefficient. In order to optimize, ITIL V3 recommends integrating Request Fulfillment with Service Catalog. This transforms static display of IT services into an actionable self-service tool useful to both business users and IT and this results in the introduction of Actionable service catalog.

Sample service catalog as viewed by your end users

Below is the end user view of a sample service catalog.

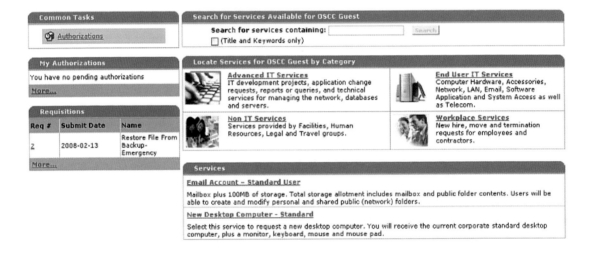

Internal view of your service catalog

Below is the internal view of your service catalog.

Search for Service Offerings

Search for Service Offering Containing [   ] [Search]
☐ (Title and Keywords only)

Locate Service Offerings by Category

Application Services
Hosting, support and maintenance and enhancement of existing and new applications.
- Application Management
- Quotes - Hosting New Applications

Support Services
Front line support for users of personal computing, applications, networking, communication and other technologies.
- Service Desk
- Training

Infrastructure Services
Services that offer the business fundamental technical infrastructure components such as the wide area network and telecommunication backbone.
- IT Management
- Network

Workplace Services
Provides a full range of personal computing services designed to make employees productive.
- Email and Collaboration
- Voice Services
- Workstations

Professional Services
Offers a full set of consulting services for each phase of an IT deployment from assessment and implementation right through to upgrade planning.
- Other Consulting
- Project Consulting

Other Services
Provides support for miscellaneous IT services and services outside the IT domain such as Facilities, Human Resources, Travel, and Legal.
- Non-IT Services
- Other IT Services

Filter Service Offerings by Fiscal Year [All ▾]

EMAIL & COLLABORATION (2007)

Provides secure access to corporate email account and collaborative scheduling capabilities. Packages are available for Standard Users, Power Users who require expanded storage and add-ons such as wireless access, and Light Users who only occasionally access email.

You can easily add packaged options - such as instant messaging, NetMeeting, spam control, and BlackBerry wireless access - to any package. We've streamlined the delivery process, making it easier to map your requirements to our capabilities, and then accelerate the implementation timeframe.

It's everything you need to deliver the kind of globally available, secure mail and communications solution that your users demand - and that your adaptive enterprise needs to stay agile in the face of ever-present change.

Personal Computing (2008)   Initiate Agreement

The Personal Computing service provides end-to-end lifecycle support for company desktops and laptops. It includes a portfolio of essential services required to deliver an efficient and reliable personal computing environment for business users while protecting company assets/data, and controlling support costs by leveraging consistent service management best practices.

The Personal Computing service includes provisioning a leased desktop or laptop for a monthly subscription fee, desk-side field support services and ongoing move, change and disposal services for supported computing equipment.

CHAPTER 14

Build a remote backup service offering. Try Amazon S3.

Two reasons why you should offer remote backup

Sources say that 40% of companies that don't have disaster recovery plans go out of business in the event of a storm or any other natural calamity. That's the number one reason why you should offer remote backups. It ensures business continuity to your customers at some of time when nature strikes. Secondly, the tools that do automated backups have improved a lot making it really hassle free to build a service offering on top of them without making any significant investment.

In-house backup Vs remote backup

Many of you might face this situation when you try to sell your own remote backup services. Your customer already runs an in house backup either on a tape or a disc. But don't panic, there are some interesting facts that help you convert such customers to your remote backup service. Reports say that of the companies that do in house backup there are lot of chances for things to go wrong as discussed below.

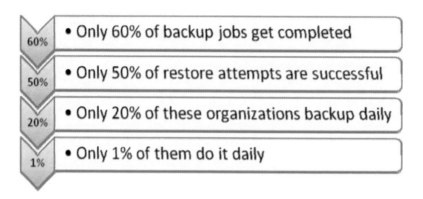

- 60% • Only 60% of backup jobs get completed
- 50% • Only 50% of restore attempts are successful
- 20% • Only 20% of these organizations backup daily
- 1% • Only 1% of them do it daily

How to build a remote backup service offering

The options available to you can be broadly categorized into two – 1) simple reselling of someone's backup service where the data resides in the vendor's datacenter and 2) building the service all by yourself - buy backup software and store data yourself.

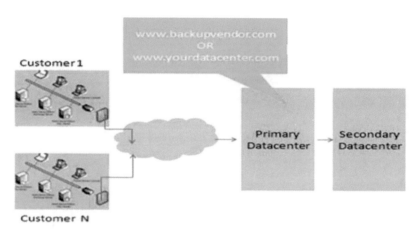

Backup vendors

Some of the popular backup vendors who offer solutions to Managed Service Providers:

Vendor	Details
Ahsay www.ahsay.com	Ahsay™ Backup Software Service Provider Edition allows you to fully brand the software into your own label and to be part of your total data protection and disaster recovery solution. Portal enables you to brand the client software, management console, and backup job reports on the fly.
Vembu StoreGrid www.vembu.com	StoreGrid helps you to backup your clients data to a server managed by you or to a cloud computing and storage platform like computing.

(Continue)

(Continued)

Secure Resolutions www.secureresoultions.com	ResolutionsMSP Backup and Data Recovery support local backups as well as those over the Internet to their secured datacenters. All data is encrypted on disk and in transit.
Remote Backups www.remotedatabackups.com	Remote Backups provides easy to use, secure and reliable backup solution that takes backups of the data and stores in their secured data centers and mirrored.
Compu Vault www.compuvault.com	CompuVault automatically and securely backs up all your data - data that resides on every machine on your LAN, if required. And it backs it up directly to the offsite storage vault in a secure data center, requiring no daily user interaction. CompuVault's data backup and recovery services are automated and centrally managed to help you protect your critical data.
Storagecraft www.storagecragt.com	StorageCraft's wide range of products that offer disaster recovery, disk backup, data protection and security solutions. Managed Service Provider (MSP) offers Partner Program to give MSPs, VARs and other resellers a way to sell ShadowProtect™ disk-based backup and disaster recovery as a managed service.
Backup Solutions www.backupsolutions.com	BackUp Solutions provides online backup services which are secure, automated and easy to use. They have professionally managed, mirrored and highly redundant data centers with a 99.9% historical uptime over the last seven years to ensure 24/7 availability of their customers' files whenever they need them.
NovaBACKUP us.novastar.com	NovaBACKUP Business Essentials provides data protection software solution for small and medium businesses and protects all their critical information.
IASO Backup technology www.iasobackup.com	IASO Backup Bank offers you a full online backup service solution, at a fixed monthly rate. Your data is backed up via Internet to our highly secured datacenter, offering the backup functionality and service level your organization requires.
Storage Guardian www.storagegaurdian.com	Storage Guardian is a complete, secure, on-line data management service for enterprise-wide LANs, including automated backup, fault-tolerant off-site storage, and fast data recovery.
Asigra www.asigra.com	Asigra Televaulting is completely integrated to support your business. Asigra Televaulting for Service Providers is a WAN platform solution for delivering backup/restore service as a utility. It incorporates everything you need to deploy, provision, and start selling your storage service.
Iron Mountain www.ironmountain.com	Iron Mountain's LiveVault is a complete server data backup and recovery solution for remote offices of large enterprises and small & medium-sized businesses. Combining proven disk and online technologies, LiveVault radically simplifies the protection of all your company's servers, including file, database, application and Exchange servers - virtually eliminating the risks and burdens of traditional backup methods.

Amazon S3

Amazon's Simple Storage Service (S3) provides cheap and unlimited online data storage for anyone with a credit card and an Amazon Web Service (AWS) account. If you have an AWS account, you can interact with the S3 service using specialized tools to upload and manage your files. Amazon says that the same scalable storage infrastructure that powers amazon.com is the one that powers S3.

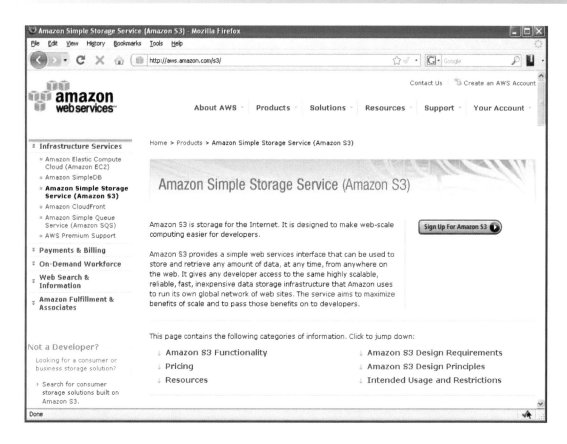

S3 adoption is growing

Since its inception in March 2006 lot of companies have started using S3. The number of buckets (unit of storage) in S3 has almost tripled in the last one year. Photo hosting service SmugMug is believed to have saved more than a million dollar by using S3 instead of their dedicated storage servers. Lots of storage vendors have started using S3 and other Amazon services. Good example is Vembu Store Grid Backup Software which offers EC2/S3 support in its upcoming version.

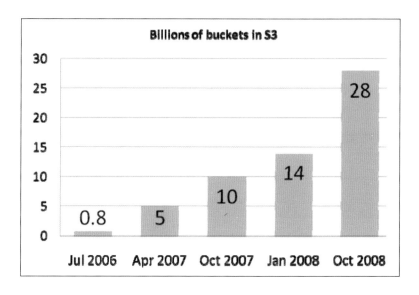

How it works?

It stores everything as an object, each not more than 5 gigabytes in size. These objects are organized into buckets and identified within each bucket by a unique user-assigned key. Buckets and objects can be created, listed, and retrieved using a HTTP interface (REST) or SOAP interface.

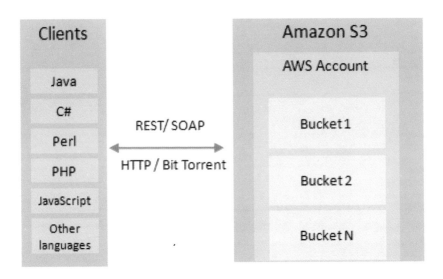

Pricing

At $0.15 per gigabyte per month Amazon is the most inexpensive online storage option available today. Amazon wants you to pay for the storage, the bandwidth you (and your users) consume, and for the number of requests you send to its servers.

	Storage Per GB for first 50TB	Bandwidth Per GB (in/out)	Requests Per 1,000
United States	$0.15	$0.1 / $0.17	$0.01
Europe	$0.18	$0.1 / $0.17	$0.012

CHAPTER 15

Reducing Hosting Cost with Amazon

If you are a start-up managed service provider, I would recommend you taking a look at Amazon Web Services. It is very promising and it helps you host your software on Amazon EC2 (Elastic Compute Cloud), store the data on a networked drive EBS (Elastic Block Store), and backup the data on to the S3 (Simple Storage Service) with an uptime guarantee of 99.95%. All this for less than $99 per month.

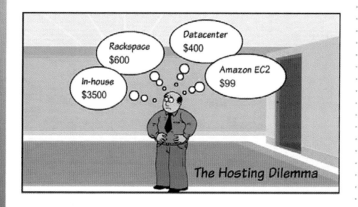

Key Components in Amazon Web Services

How EC2 works?

How EBS works

Elastic IP Address – for redundancy

How Amazon EC2 differs from Traditional Data Centers

Key Components in Amazon Web Services

Amazon cloud basically has three components you need to know about:

- EC2: *Elastic Compute Cloud* (your server in the clouds)
- EBS: *Elastic Block Store* (your disk drive in the clouds)
- S3: *Simple Storage Service* (your storage platform in the clouds)

How EC2 works?

EC2 works on Xen virtualization technology. Each virtual server is called a server instance and available in various sizes. Sizes are defined based on EC2 compute units, which is the equivalent of CPU capacity of a physical hardware. EC2 now supports the following operating systems - Red Hat Enterprise Linux, Oracle Enterprise Linux, Windows Server 2003, OpenSolaris, Fedora, Debian, Cent OS, Gentoo Linux and FreeBSD.

EC2 Instance Options

Instance Size	No. of EC2 units*	Memory equivalent	Hard disk equivalent	Processor Platform
Small	1	1.7 GB	160 GB	32 bit
Large	4	7.5 GB	850 GB	64 bit
Extra Large	8	15 GB	1690 GB	64 bit
High CPU Instance				

(Continue)

(Continued)

| High CPU Medium Instance | 5 | 1.7 GB | 350 GB | 32 bit |
| High CPU Extra Large Instance | 20 | 7 GB | 1690 GB | 64 bit |

* 1 EC2 Compute Unit = 1.0-1.2 GHz 2007 Opteron or 2007 Xeon processor

EC2 Pricing

Instances	Windows (US)	Linux/Unix (US)	Linux/Unix (Europe)
Small	$0.125/hr	$0.1/hr	$0.11/hr
Large	$0.5/hr	$0.4/hr	$0.44/hr
Extra Large	$1/hr	$0.8/hr	$0.88/hr
High CPU Medium Instance	$0.3/hr	$0.2/hr	$0.22/hr
High CPU Extra Large Instance	$1.2/hr	$0.8/hr	$0.88/hr

Note: Amazon does not support Windows based applications in Europe region.

How EBS works

EC2 provides the option to store the data of the instances on Amazon Elastic Block Store (EBS), an off-instance storage device (similar to that of a hard disk). EBS is independent of the life of the instances; thereby you can keep your data redundant. Amazon EBS volumes are highly available, reliable and are attached to EC2 instances and are exposed as standard block devices. EBS volumes offer greatly improved durability over local EC2 instance stores, as Amazon automates backup for EBS volumes. Not limiting with EBS and automated backups Amazon offers much more durability by providing the option to store the EBS volumes on Amazon S3 as snapshots and thereby replicating the data across multiple availability zones. Amazon does not encrypt the data while storing it in EBS, but recommends to having an encrypted file system on top of the EBS.

Amazon EBS Volumes	Price in US	Price in Europe
Per GB of provisioned storage per month	$0.1	$0.11
Per 1 million I/O requests	$0.1	$0.11

Amazon EBS to S3	Price in US	Price in Europe
Per GB of data stored per month	$0.15	$0.18
Per 1000 PUT requests (when saving a snapshot)	$0.01	$0.12
Per 10,000 GET requests (when loading a snapshot)	$0.01	$0.12

Elastic IP Address – for redundancy

To make your application redundant Amazon offers Elastic IP Address, a static IP address designed for dynamic cloud computing. The big advantage with Elastic IP Address is that you need not depend on a technician to replace the host, or wait for DNS to switch to all of your customers when a particular instance goes down, you can programmatically remap to another instance, provided you have another instance running already. An Elastic IP Address is associated with your account and not with a single instance, you can obtain one and use whenever you require. However, Amazon charges $0.1/hr when you are not using due to the limited availability of public IPs and for effective usage.

Elastic IP Address	Price in US	Price in Europe
Per non attached Elastic IP Address per complete hour (when not using)	$0.01	$0.01
First 100 remaps/month per Elastic IP Address remap	$0.00	$0.00
More than 100 remaps/month per Elastic IP Address remap	$0.1	$0.1

Data Transfer: Accessing EC2

Pricing also varies according to the data transferred in and out of the instances. Data transferred between two Amazon Web Services within the same region (i.e. between Amazon EC2 US and another AWS service in the US, or between Amazon EC2 Europe and another AWS service in Europe) is free of charge. Data transferred between AWS services in different regions will be charged as Internet Data Transfer on both sides of the transfer. However, usage for other Amazon Web Services like S3 is billed separately from Amazon EC2.

Data Transfer IN	Price
All data transfer	$0.1/GB
Data Transfer OUT	Price
First 10TB per month	$0.17/GB
Next 40TB per month	$0.13/GB
Next 100TB per month	$0.11/GB
Over 150TB per month	$0.10/GB

Amazon charges $0.01 per GB in/out for all the data transferred between instances in different availability zones in the same region i.e., data transferred by an instance in an availability location in California to another instance in Florida.

How Amazon EC2 differs from Traditional Data Centers

Amazon EC2	Traditional Data Centers
Pay only for what you use	Fixed cost for the resources you use
Billing is calculated on hourly basis	Billing calculated on predetermined fixed period
Easily scale up or down whenever required	Number of resources is fixed and difficult to handle sudden computing requirements
Full control on your computing resources. You can launch/terminate instances whenever required.	Full control over the computing resources is not provided.

AWS Console and Elastic Fox

Amazon offers two User Interfaces for you to manage your instances. One is the http://console.aws.amazon.com and other is a firefox add-on.

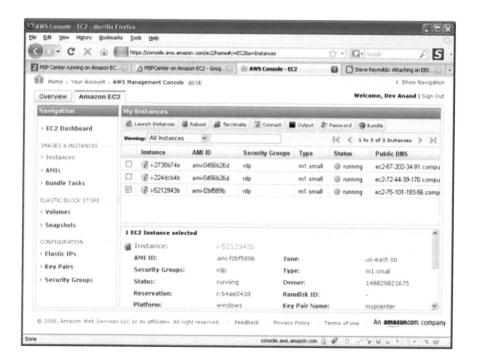

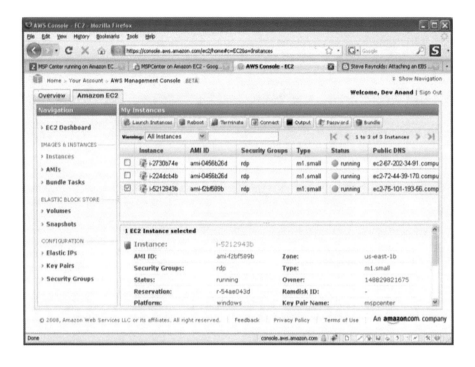

Hosting MSP Center Plus on Amazon Cloud

You can now run MSP Center Plus software on the Amazon cloud. For your convenience we have created an Amazon Machine Instance (AMI) of MSP Center Plus. This instance consists of a fresh copy of MSP Center running on a 32bit Windows 2003 R2 Datacenter Edition with 1.7GB RAM.

Steps to run MSP Center Plus on Amazon EC2 + EBS

Amazon doesn't preserve the state of any of its EC2 instances, which means if an instance crashes your data is lost forever. To solve this problem you can store DATA and other CONFIG files of MSP Center Plus on an EBS volume which has better reliability (at least 10 times more than a conventional drive) so that during a crash you can launch a new instance within minutes and associate the EBS volume to it.

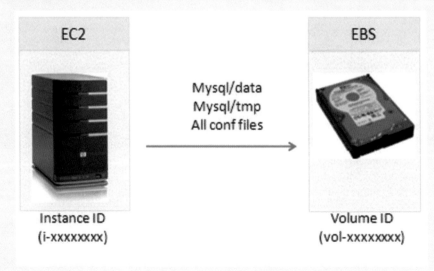

Steps to run EC2 + EBS

1. Get an AWS account - www.amazon.com/gp/aws/registration/registration-form.html
2. Sign in to AWS Console - https://console.aws.amazon.com
3. Choose AMIs and search for an AMI named mspcenter (mspcenter/mspcenter.manifest.xml).
4. Run the instance (note down the instance id i-xxxxxxxx).

You have now successfully started your MSP Center Plus on EC2. Now you need to configure MSP Center Plus to store data on to an EBS so that your data is safe.

1. Create EBS volume: In the AWS console choose VOLUMES. Create a new volume and attach it with your instance (that id you noted in step4 above).
2. RDP to your virtual machine with the default password oklgJordv1.
3. Launch the diskmgmt.msc (start->run->discmgmt.msc). Find the Amazon disc at the bottom of this wizard and follow instructions on screen. Name the new drive as E. Any other alphabet would require other changes in configuration so name it as E.
4. Configuring MSP Center to store data into that drive
   1. Stop MSP Center Plus.
   2. Copy mysql/data and mysql/tmp folders from C:\ProgramFiles\AdventNet\ME\Central\ to E:\data and E:tmp
   3. Start MSP Center Plus.

Steps to restore your installation if MSP Center machine crashes

In case of a server crash you can restore your setup by doing the following

1. Launch a new instance of MSP Center.
2. Go to Volumes tab and attach your volume with the new instance.
3. RDP to your machine and ensure that you don't format the drive.
4. Open E:\mspconfbacku.bkf and restore it over C:\programfiles\adventnet\me\central\
5. Start MSP Center Plus.

Steps to run MSP Center Plus on Amazon EC2 + EBS + S3

If you feel that even EBS is not so secure you can back up the EBS in S3 so that in case of a failure of EBS you can restore the S3 data into a new EBS volume.

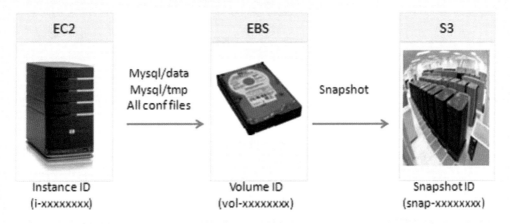

Steps to backup your EBS data to S3

If you wish to take a backup of your EBS volume to S3 do the following

1. Go to Volumes tab in your AWS console and CREATE SNAPSHOT.

Steps to restore your S3 snapshot into EBS

At times if your EBS drive fails you can restore it back from the snapshot you created in S3. Steps for that

1. Go to volumes tab in your AWS console and create new volume.
2. Choose the snapshot id from the list.
3. Create.
4. Follow steps to associate the volume with your instance.

CHAPTER 16

Make friends with SAAS. Resell Google Apps / Zoho.

Journey of messaging and collaboration tools

If there is one thing that you can always sell to any new business, that's E-Mail. No company can do without that. I am sure most of you would have tons of experience in email and messaging tools such as Microsoft Exchange and IBM Lotus Notes. These been the de-facto vendors for many long years. But today we have some inexpensive players with interesting technologies such as Software-as-a-service (SAAS) that offer similar functionality. We recommend you to take a look at these players and check if they are the new age email tools for your next breed of customers.

Google Apps

Google offers business e-mail, messaging, document management, and information sharing through SAAS. Google receives 3000 registrations every day for Google apps and more than a million organizations have registered so far. Google apps are available in two standard and premium editions. The standard edition includes only Email & calendar, storage for mails, docs and sites and offered at free of cost for individual users and universities. Premium edition includes Email & Calendar, Email storage (25GB), 99.9% uptime SLA, docs and sites, video, storage for mails and docs etc.

Benefit of SAAS

Traditional business applications such as Microsoft Exchange, Microsoft Office, and Microsoft SharePoint cost more when compared to this SAAS model. For example to setup a highly available email system for your customers it takes $300-$1000 per user per year. But with Google you can get it for $50 per user per year. You can make use of SAAS and explain your customers the benefits that they can gain using it. Google has been sending targeted messages to solution providers asking them to switch from legacy systems to efficient SAAS based Google apps. One such video titled **Becoming a Google Apps Solution Provider** is available in YouTube which everyone should take a look.

Zoho Apps

Zoho offers Productivity & Collaboration apps and Business apps as SAAS. Productivity & Collaboration tools include E-mail, docs, chat etc. while Business apps include CRM, project management, online database etc. Zoho also offers the above services at free of cost to individual users and universities and charges $50 per user/year for enterprises.

Google Vs Zoho

	Google	Zoho
Word Processor	Google Docs	Zoho Writer
Spreadsheet	Google spreadsheet	Zoho Sheet
PowerPoint Presentations	Google Presentation	Zoho Show
Web Clippings	Google Notebook	Zoho Notebook
Email	Gmail	Zoho Mail
Chat	Google Talk	Zoho chat
Wiki	(Google acquired JotSpot)	Zoho Wiki
Database Application	--	Zoho Creator
Online Database	--	Zoho DB
Project Management	--	Zoho Projects
Web conferencing	(Google acquired Marratech)	Zoho Meeting
Customer Relationship Management (CRM)	--	Zoho CRM
Personal Organizer	--	Zoho Planner
Web hosting	Google Page Creator	--
Feed Reader	Google Reader	--

CHAPTER 17

How to retain customers?

Stop the leaky bucket model

It doesn't make sense if you win five customers every quarter and lose four. As you are building a business over a recurring revenue model, such leaky bucket approach of losing customers is extremely dangerous. Moreover, with rising competition and deepening recession, it is going to be ten times more expensive to acquire a new customer than to retain one. So better learn how to retain your customers.

Four reasons why customers switch managed service providers

An Adage in Business management is that bad experiences teach you the best lessons. That's why many MBA case studies focuses on what went wrong. Today, running a successful managed services business depends on having strong partnerships with your customers. According to analysts, the major reasons why customers switch managed service providers are:

Top reasons why customers switch	Description
Improper Packaging	The first problem the managed service providers face is packaging. They are merely renaming their maintenance or outsourcing capabilities rather than offering genuine managed services. Others are creating complicated managed service portfolios that confuse potential customers.
Pricing	The second issue is pricing. Rather than providing a simple fee schedule for their managed services, many providers have created complex pricing algorithms that frustrate prospective customers.
Positioning	The third challenge is positioning these services properly. In most cases, managed services are simply promoted as a way to reduce staff and lower operating costs. While these benefits are essential, few managed service providers can clearly differentiate themselves or show how they add value to their customers.
Poor salesmanship	But the biggest obstacle to selling managed services is poor sales skills. Many managed service providers rely on traditional, transaction-oriented salespeople to sell managed services. These salespeople generally are good at selling relatively standardized products or services but inexperienced at selling ongoing managed service relationships. Rather than simply selling the cost savings of managed services, salespeople must learn how to convince their enterprise customers of the potential business value of their offerings.

Customer survey – a great tool to retain customers

Though there is no magic to retain customers you can still bet on age old techniques such as periodic customer survey to gauge their satisfaction levels and take remedial actions before they disappear. Customer Surveys are very essential to identify customer satisfaction, requirements, demands etc. These surveys allow your customers to give their concerns and appreciations on the services and support you offer. The more number of customers praise and the less they demand from you, puts your level top in the market and vice versa. Benefits of Periodical Customer Survey

- Know whether your customers are satisfied or not
- Shows where you stand in the market
- Understand your customers demands/requirements
- Know what your competitors offer
- Continual Improvement Process

Automated customer survey

Many MSP platforms today offer automated and periodic customer survey module integrated into ticketing system. For example, with MSP Center Plus you can create a satisfaction survey and automatically send it everytime a customer ticket is closed or for every nth mailer from a customer is closed etc. The reports will give you the overall picture of how satisfied your customers are.

CHAPTER 18

How to build a motivated team?

Single essential ingredient

People are the single most essential ingredient to any organization's success and in managed services that is the number one factor. Basically you are converting a hands-for-rent business into a process oriented and efficient business and that makes building a dynamic and efficient team very critical in ensuring success. Most importantly, these cross functional teams should function as one so that they become an extension to the client's IT team and not just another company doing some break fixes. The teams should be motivated, agile, and productive. Without setting up this team there is no scope for success whatever you do.

Case study — What a young and motivated team can do?

We have a customer in Austin where the average age of their Managed Services Team is 23 (excluding their solutions architect and the head of managed services who are very well experienced but if included in the equation would increase the average age by another 10-15 years !!!).

This company is an extended IT division of the world's leading defense vendor. They manage medium and large enterprises with annual revenues of at least $50-100 million or above. I have spent couple of days with them observing how they use our platform (MSP Center Plus) and how they serve their customers every day. I should say I was amazed. They can beat any technical challenge thrown to them hands down. They know every tool in the world that makes their life better. They can drill down to the problem and fix it before it affects their customers. And it's quite unbelievable to see that such a young team holds the responsibility of managing some of the world's well known and large customers.

Setup a test lab for your engineers to try new things

For IT guys mounted with routine mundane tasks get bored up quite often. They have a heart for working on cutting edge technology and trying new things and it is important that you provide them with a test lab environment to play around. This kills boredom and also helps them hone their skills every now and then.

CHAPTER 19

Which is better?
Hosted or In-house?

Hosted or In-house

With the advent of SAAS, the key question in every-body's mind is this – what should I choose? Hosted solution or In-house one? We have seen different stories from each camp and to be honest there are advantages and disadvantages in each model. The SAAS model for example is a near turn-key solution. It takes away most of the installation and other headaches but gets very expensive as you grow.

See the table below, it's the pricing sheet by a Hosted MSP vendor (securemycompany.com).

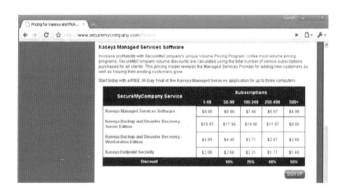

Now, let's compare this pricing with an in-house software vendor such as MSP Center Plus. The annual out go for you for these solutions would be as given below.

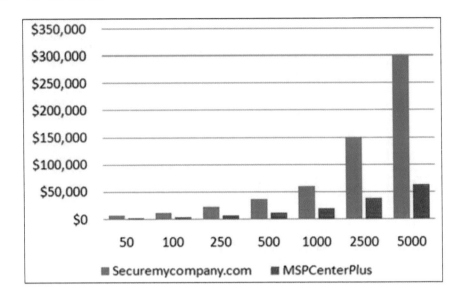

# devices	Securemycompany.com	MSP Center Plus
50	$5,970	$1,250
100	$10,752	$2,500
250	$22,380	$5,500
500	$35,820	$10,500
1000	$59,760	$18,000
2500	$149,400	$37,500
5000	$298,800	$62,500

Verdict: Start with hosted solutions to test the market and then move to packaged software as you grow beyond 100 devices.

CHAPTER 20

Which is better? Multiple tools or integrated tool?

Disparate tools Vs Integrated MSP Platform

Most MSPs don't think long term and start using disparate tools for every need. This chaotic behavior ends up in reducing productivity of the teams and also hampers growth. That's where integrated MSP platforms such as MSP Center Plus score high. These platforms offer all the essential remote management functionalities in a single UI.

Disparate tools Vs
Integrated MSP Platform

Integration is the
way to go

Criteria	Multiple tools	Integrated tool
Cost	High. Costs more as you buy more tools.	Low. Costs less as you buy a single tool.
Data integration	Lacks data integration. Data is spread across multiple tools and often results in information silos.	Data is integrated. Easy to access.
Time to resolution	Finding resolution consumes more time.	Less time consuming.
User experience	Tiring & unpleasant as the user have to use multiple UIs.	All under single UI.
Control	No Control as there is any record of who did what.	Complete control as users login to the same UI.

Integration is the way to go

Integrated offerings are not only COOL but are inexpensive and offer excellent productivity and less hurdle in maintenance than a mix of tools.

	Other RMM Tools	Other PSA Tools	MSP Center Plus
Device monitoring	✓	✗	✓
Remote Control	✓	✗	✓
Patch management	✓	✗	✓
SLA management	✓	✗	✓
Desktop management	✓	✗	✓
Asset management	✓	✗	✓
Helpdesk	✗	✓	✓
Service Automation	✗	✓	✓
Technician scheduling	✗	✓	✓
Timesheet & invoice creation	✗	✓	✓
Cost	**$120***	**>$5000**	**$25***

Unleash the MSP in you.
Good luck.

www.mspcenterplus.com

Made in the USA
Lexington, KY
23 December 2009